GW00993993

SATHYA SAI'S

AMRITA VARSHINI

(NECTAR SHOWERS)

SUDHA ADITYA

PUBLISHING

First Edition, 1992
Second Edition, 1996
Reprint, 1997 1998

ISBN-81-86822-07-0

Published & Distributed by :
Sai Towers Publishing
(A Unit of Sri Sathya Sai Towers Hotels Pvt Ltd.)
3/497 Main Road
Prasanthi Nilayam - 515 134
INDIA
Tel   : 91-8555-87880
Fax   : 91-8555-87302
EMail   : saitower@giasbg01.vsnl.net.in

Contact for Mail Order in U.S.A.
JAI SAI RAM
PO Box 900
Trinidad, CO 81082 U.S.A.
Phone   : (719) 846-0846
Fax   : (719) 846-0847
E-Mail   : jaisairm @ ria.net
             OR
jaisairm @ rmi.net

Printed by :
D.K. Fine Arts Press Pvt. Ltd.
New Delhi - 110 052

DIVINE MESSAGE

Whatever be your fate or destiny,

Joy or strife, peace or mutiny;

Turn to Me with faith complete

And cling to Me with love replete,

Shower I Blessings in profusion -

AMRITA VARSHINI of Compassion!

- Bhagavan Sri Sathya Sai Baba.

A PRAYER

O'Lord! Take my love and let it flow in fullness of
devotion to Thee.

O'Lord! Take my hands and let them work incessantly
for Thee.

O'Lord! Take my soul and let it be merged in one with
Thee.

O'Lord! Take my mind, thoughts, words and deeds and
let them be in tune with Thee.

O'Lord! Take my everything and let me be Thy
instrument to work.

I do but aspire to grow
In longing for Thy Lotus-Feet;
And to sing Thy Holy Name
With every breath of my being.

Sudha Aditya.

CONTENTS

PREFACE

Our Beloved Sai first drew me to His Lotus Feet in 1978. After this, He initiated me into meditation and also blessed me with the ability to receive messages from Him during my dhyana sessions. I was thrilled and overjoyed at this overwhelming sign of Grace, but the human mind being what it is, I began to harbour doubts about the "messages". Were they figments of my imagination or expressions of my subconscious mind? I therefore prayed hard and sincerely to Him to clear my uncertainty and remove my doubts. Our Sai is a boundless ocean of love and compassion and He instantly responded to the pleas of a beseeching heart. One night, He granted me His Darsan in a dream, in which He confirmed the authenticity of the messages. He indicated beyond doubt that I was indeed receiving them from Him. He also cautioned me not to misuse the power of direct communication. "Don't waste it on worldly problems. Confine it to the spiritual, as far as possible", He said.

Since then He has been constantly instructing and guiding me through the Inner Voice. He has given me beautiful elucidations on life, truth and spiritualism in the form of prose and poetry. I have been recording some of His teachings in the form of "Conversations". A couple of months ago, I received His Divine Command that I should share them with fellow devotees. He instructed me to publish some of His teachings in book-form and to name the book "Sathya Sai's Amrita Varshini". His teachings are indeed like nectar showers, drenching the inner spirit with love and bliss. Dear Sai brothers and sisters, I hope you will enjoy reading this book and will benefit by its teachings.

I humbly dedicate this book to the Lotus Feet of Our Beloved Bhagavan and remain, ever sincerely in Sai prema and seva.

Sudha Aditya
Madras

vi

SILENCE AND THE INNER VOICE

SAI - The Inner Voice, *Antar Vani*, is the Voice of the Sadguru or the Divine Voice. It is incorporated in the *Ajna Chakra** which has its focal point in the *bhrumadhya* region; that is, in the region of the third eye or the eyebrow centre. When this *chakra* is awakened and the *Kundalini* energy ascends to it, the Inner -Voice or the Guru's Voice can be heard. In order to awaken the Kundalini *shakti* and make it rise to the *Ajna Chakra*, you have to concentrate on this *chakra*, in the *bhrumadhya*. You have to sharpen your concentration to a very fine degree and shut out all other sensations, feelings, thoughts and emotions. Then, in the void, can be heard the Inner Voice. It can be heard only in the state of mindlessness.

I shall give you a small example. In your radio, you have various frequencies and wavelengths. Each transmitting station is tuned to a particular wave length. If you want a particular station, you tune in to that particular band or wavelength through which it transmits. It cannot be heard on any other band. Thus you have medium-wave bands and shortwave bands. But you also have a FM band which is a high frequency modulation. It is a special band which exists on a special frequency modulation. When you tune into this FM band, the transmission is loud and clear without any outside disturbances. On the other hand, when you tune into the shortwave bands, stations often overlap and the result is discordant noise and confusion.

Now, the *Ajna Chakra* is like the FM band and all the lower *chakras* are like medium and shortwave bands. When you tune in to *Ajna Chakra* (FM), all other frequencies, waves and disturbances are cut off and the Inner Voice comes through clear, strong and true. Of course, the strength and clarity of *Antar Vani* depends on your fine-tuning, that is your concentration and your ability to reach the state of *shoonyam* (void) or mindlessness.

However, it is not enough if you merely "hear" the Inner Voice. More importantly, you should "listen" to It - follow It's advice and carry out It's instructions implicitly and unquestioningly, because the advice and instructions are those of the Divine Sadguru. It is only when you "listen" to and "obey" the Voice that you will find peace and happiness.

S - How would You explain the fine-tuning, Baba?

SAI - Fine-tuning is the degree of your concentration.

There are three stages in concentration. In the first stage, you receive My messages in the form of thought waves. In the second stage, you can hear My own Voice and in the third stage, you can hear My Voice as well as see me. With successful *Chitha-Suddhi* (purification of the mind), you will be able to progress from stage to stage.

S- Baba, there are some people who do not practise Kundalini Yoga, yet they are able to experience the Inner Voice.

SAI - Of course, why not? I have already told you that when the mind is still and silent, the Voice of God can be heard. The mind is like a switch. If you turn it to the right, towards God, you can tune in to God. If you turn it to the left, you tune in to the world. God is present everywhere and in everyone. He is *Sarvaantaryami*. The question is not whether He can make Himself heard; the question is whether you have the ability to hear Him. Anyone who has the ability to clear the mind of disquiet, unrest, thoughts and conflicts and is able to keep the mind in a state of silent equilibrium, can tune in to the Inner Voice of God. After all, silence is God. When the heart and mind are silent, you can experience God.

Here, I shall tell you briefly about "*mauna*" which means silence. What is *mauna?* The word "*mauna*" consists of two syllables, "ma" and "na". "Ma" is "*manas*" (mind) and "na" is "*nahi*" (no). So, "*mauna*" means the state where there is no mind. When can you say that there is no mind or that the mind ceases to exist? When it is not disturbed by emotions, desires, feelings, thoughts, etc. When the mind ceases to exist, you can experience God.

Really speaking, it is most desirable to be in a constant state of *mauna*; then you can enjoy the constant presence of God. So, begin to practise *mauna* right from today. Practise *mauna* at least for half-an-hour everyday. You can observe *mauna* even while going about your daily chores. When the tongue is active, the ears are also alert for responses and you absorb all sorts of vibrations which affect the mind adversely, the mind cannot be calm and still. But when the tongue is quiet, the ears are unresponsive and the mind is not affected by external factors, the mind becomes calm and quiet and you will be able to experience a sense of deep peace within yourself.

When the mind is peaceful and silent, you also have extra energy. Instead of wasting your energy on meaningless irritations and annoyances, you will be able to channel the energy in the right directions. You will be able to think better and work better. So, practise *mauna* for a little while everyday and see for yourself the peace and energy that can be gained.

Silence is "*Soham*", silence is "*Om*". Silence is the Voice of *Brahman*, through silence can It be known. So, practise silence in the mind and in the heart; you will thus realize the Truth, "THAT thou art".

Note:- *According to Patanjali's Yoga philosophy (in his book "*Yoga Sutras*"), there are eight chakras or wheels of energy in our body, located at various points along the spinal column. They are mooladhara, swadhisthana, manipura, anahata, visuddhi, ajna, bindu and sahasrara. Of them, mooladhara is the lowest chakra and is situated at the base of the spine; sahasrara is the highest chakra and is situated at the crown of the head. The kundalini shakti or spiritual energy is said to reside in the mooladhara chakra. Kundalini is traditionally conceived of as a coiled serpent lying dormant in the mooladhara. When kundalini awakens and ascends to the sahasrara chakra, a tremendous spiritual awakening is experienced which leads to yoga or union with God.

FAITH AND CONFIDENCE

SAI - Have confidence in Me. I shall look after everything for you.

S - Doesn't it go without saying, Baba? All your devotees have faith and confidence in You.

SAI - No. All My devotees have faith in Me, that is correct. But not all of them have confidence in Me. Faith is one thing and confidence is another thing. Only when the two exist together will there be a positive reaction from Me. If you consider a car, for example, it runs on petrol and battery. If even one of them is absent, the car will not function. For it to run without any trouble, the tank should be full of petrol and the battery should be in a good condition. Even if the tank is full but the battery is not in a proper condition, the car cannot run smoothly. It may break down and stop at any time. Repairing and restoring the battery takes a longer time than filling the tank with petrol. So, actually, the battery is more important than the petrol.

Now, faith is like the petrol and confidence is like the battery. When you have confidence in God, you will have positive battery charge. And when you are positively charged, the response from God too is immediate and positive. If you want à positive reaction or response from Me, mere faith is not sufficient. It should go hand in hand with confidence. Only then is your devotion complete - *poorna*. And when you have *poorna bhakti* or complete devotion, the response from Me will also be poorna or total.

S - What exactly do You mean by confidence, Baba? How is it different from faith?

SAI - You see, it is like this. Faith in God means faith that He is God, that He is Omnipresent, Omnipotent, Omniscient, and so on. Confidence means trust in the Word, Will and Work of God. If I say something, there is a reason; if I will something to happen, it is for a reason; if I do something, it is with reason. You should have this implicit trust - that there is always a reason for what I say, will and do. And you should have confidence in every Word and Act of Mine. Whatever I say is the truth, whatever I do is the truth, whatever I will is the truth - this is the confidence you should have, even though things may appear to be otherwise.

You must have read about the incident when Krishna and Arjuna were walking in the forest one day. Krishna looked up and saw a bird in the sky.

"Look at the bird, Arjuna", He said, "Isn't it an eagle?"
"Yes, Krishna, it's an eagle", replied Arjuna.
"No, I think it's a crow", said Krishna.
"Of course it's a crow", replied Arjuna.
"On second thoughts, it looks like a dove," He said.
"Beyond all doubt it is a dove," agreed Arjuna.

This is what implicit confidence means. You trust implicitly and blindly in the Word, Will and Act of God without any questions, doubts and uncertainties. My Word given becomes My Will. When I will something, it has to happen. Never doubt that. When I say that I will do something for you, I will certainly do it. If you have confidence in Me, it acts as a catalyst and My Will is carried out faster and quicker. Even without your confidence, My Will takes It's normal course because what I ordain will have to take place. But with your positive confidence and positive attitude, My Will gains extra energy and momentum, Do you understand?

S - Yes, Baba. It is a question of one's attitude towards God.

SAI - When you talk about attitude with regard to faith and confidence, there is a difference between your attitude towards God and God's attitude towards you. When you have faith in God, He takes you under His shelter, protects you and does not let you suffer. Here, the point is that the devotee is completely bound and God is completely free. But when the devotee shows hundred percent confidence in God, it is God who is completely bound and the devotee who is free.

S - Please explain it more explicitly, Baba.

SAI - It is like this. Each one of you has debits and credits in your *karmas* - past and present, depending upon your *samskaras* - that is your actions, thoughts, character, etc. If your *karma* is good, the result or fruit will be good. Otherwise, it will be bad. When you have bad *karma*, you have to suffer.

However, your *Faith* in God will mitigate your suffering. I give you a shot of Grace which acts as a drug or a painkiller. In short, when you have hundred percent faith, God in His Compassion reduces your suffering but He cannot reduce your karmas. Your karmas act as brakes and are binding on you. All the Lord does is to hand out Grace according to your karmas, according to what you deserve. In this way, you are bound and the Lord is entirely free.

But, when you show cent percent *Confidence* in God, He is totally bound to take care of you. No *karmas* of yours, whether good or bad can stand in the way and act as brakes. When you show such implicit confidence in God and the unshakable belief that "He will take care of everything for me, so why should I worry?" then He can never let you down. He has to look after you and take care of everything for you, come what may, and whatever be the circumstances of your *karmas* or *samskaras*. In this way, God is fully bound by His obligation to the devotee and the devotee in his turn is free.

The power of total confidence is so great that it transgresses all *karmas*. It has the power of tying up God and completely binding Him in golden fetters, so that He is forced to bow down to the devotee and accede to his wishes and wants.

Hundred percent faith means that God will not let you suffer, hundred percent confidence means that God will not let you down. Hundred percent faith plus hundred percent confidence makes for hundred percent devotion or *bhakti*. It is the highest form of bhakti-parabhakti - where the Lord is in a state of golden bondage and the devotee is in a state of supreme serenity and smiling freedom. This is what every devotee has to aim at.

You must remember here that faith and confidence are not two separate emotions. Without faith, there can be no confidence. If you do not have faith in someone, how can you have trust and confidence in him? So, faith comes first and then comes confidence. Faith is the seed, confidence is the sprout and devotion is the fruit.

S - Swami, sometimes You say that You will do something "tomorrow" but that "tomorrow" occurs after several years. Why is that?

SAI - Well, my child, you will not be able to understand it completely. It is enough for you to know that I am *Kaalateeta* - above and beyond Time. So I am not bound by earthly time limits and measurements. My conception of Time is different from yours. You are in a cage and to you, Time is measured by days and nights, hours and minutes. But I am outside the cage. I am in Eternal Light, and Time to Me is Eternal. I am not restricted by days, months or years. Everything, whether past, present or future, is the same to Me. All Time is the present. Every Time is NOW. I see things in a different way from you because My perspective or *drishti* is different.

S - To sum up, then ....

SAI - To sum up, your faith should give you total confidence in Me. You should have the implicit confidence that I will look after you, take care of you and provide for you. You should have the confidence that My Grace is always with you and that I am always watching over you and protecting you. You should have the confidence that I will never let you down, that I am always there beside you, helping you, supporting you, comforting you and carrying you through troubles and hardships. Just as you lean against the wall knowing that it will not collapse, lean on Me and depend upon Me entirely. I will then look after you and take care of everything for you. As Krishna said in the *Bhagavad Gita*, it will be *"Yogakshemam Vahaamyaham"**. That is, if you depend upon Me with complete faith and confidence, I shall provide for your welfare and look after all your needs in this world and in the next.

Note :- *Lord Krishna declared in the ninth chapter of the *Bhagavad Gita* - "Whoever among devotees dedicates all acts to Me, with no other thought, whoever meditates on Me, serves Me, worships Me, remembers Me and knows that I am always with him, ever providing for him, I bear all his burdens and guarantee fulfilment of his needs and security".

SATHWIC FOOD AND FASTING

SAI - Do you know how important the intake of food is to a *sadhaka*? To begin with, food is of three types - *rajasic, tamasic* and *sathwic*.*

Rajasic foods are those which are too hot, too spicy and too rich. They increase the rajasic nature of man and produce qualities like extreme anger, pride, conceit, egoism, arrogance, etc.

Tamasic foods are those which are stale, insipid, too salty, too sour, too bitter and twice cooked food. They aggravate the tamasic qualities like sleep, sloth and laziness and the baser qualities like desire, hankering, etc.

On the other hand, *sathwic* foods are the balanced and moderate foods which are neither too hot nor too spicy, neither *rajasic* nor *tamasic*. They sit lightly in the stomach, do not cause digestive disorders and enable easy elimination. They do not affect the mind adversely. On the contrary, they induce a state of peace and tranquillity which are very essential for *dhyana* and *sadhana*.

I shall give you an example to illustrate how non-sathwic foods affect the mind. Bheeshma, the grand sire of the Kauravas and the Pandavas was a very wise, learned and enlightened man. Everyone had immense respect and veneration for him because he always adhered to *dharma* (righteousness) and lived by his high *dharmic* principles. But what happened to all his *dharma* and wisdom when the Pandava Princes and the Princess Draupadi were being insulted and humiliated in the court of the blind King Dhritarashtra? Did Bheeshma raise his voice in protest, did he argue, did he try to put a stop when Bharatiya culture and *dharma* were being trampled in the dust by the shameful conduct of the Kauravas? No, he was silent, he felt helpless, he felt powerless. Shall I tell you why? It was because he had been eating the food of the Kauravas for years. The Kauravas were *rajasic* men, they ate rajasic food and had *rajasic* habits. Bheeshma was also eating the same food cooked in the palace kitchens. And so, in course of time, his mind was affected. He lost his clear sightedness and straight-thinking. When the hour of trial came, his mind let him down. But later, when he lay injured and dying on the battlefield of Kurukshetra, it was Arjuna's arrows which pierced his body and caused all the tainted blood to flow out. When this happened, his mind became free of delusion and tainted thoughts, his vision cleared, he regained his clarity of mind and he was able to advise the Pandavas about the principles of *dharmic* government.

So, you see how important it is to partake of the right food. *Rajasic* and *tamasic* foods contain certain undesirable and harmful chemicals which enter the body and mingle with the blood stream. In due course, the brain and the mind also get affected and they lose their purity and clarity. Therefore, every *sadhaka* should be very particular about the type of food that he eats. *Sathwic* food does not contain any dangerous chemicals and is ideal for intake.

S - Yes, Baba. I understand that the quality of food is very important.

SAI - First is quality, then comes quantity. It is not enough if you eat good quality food alone. An excess of a good thing also becomes bad; insufficiency too is bad. Eating too much is *rajasic*, eating too little is *tamasic*. But eating the proper quantity is *sathwic*. So, one should learn to eat in moderation. The main problem and defect of all mankind is that people tend to eat too much food, too much quantity. Most of the diseases of the body are caused by overeating. The body requires only a certain amount of food to function optimally and only a certain number of calories to expend energy. Anything above the required amount is eliminated. So, why should one stuff the body unnecessarily with unrequired food and invite illness? It is enough if one takes just the requisite amount of food to keep the body healthy and in good trim. One eats to live, one should not live to eat. It is better to take just that much of food which immediately appeases the hunger. Ideally, the stomach should be only three-quarters full - half with solid, quarter with water and quarter with air. Such a habit of eating will not lead to problems.

S - Is it very important to restrict the number of meals?

SAI - By all means, yes. Quality and quantity are two criteria. Then comes the number of meals. Most people have three meals, some even have four or five meals a day. This is not good at all as it creates an unnecessary burden on the stomach. Now, consider a machine in a factory. If it is working nonstop, will it not begin to malfunction? It will definitely develop faults and will break down at some time or the other. It is the same case with the stomach also. The stomach is like a machine which is responsible for the proper functioning of the digestive system. It is the main digestive organ. If it is made to work continuously for eighteen or twenty hours, it is bound to break down. If you play your tape-recorder for twelve hours a day without giving it a rest in-between, it will get overheated and will eventually stop working. The same thing will happen to the stomach if it is not given a proper rest in-between.

The *manipura* chakra is situated in the region of the stomach, behind the navel. It is the place where energy is created, stored and distributed. If this chakra does not function optimally, the entire body will be thrown out of gear. Therefore, it is also important that one eats regulated quantities at regulated times.

I have said before that those who eat thrice a day are *rogis*; those who eat twice are *bhogis*; and those who eat once a day are yogis. The stomach should not be over-loaded or over-worked. If you cannot eat just one meal a day, at least try to develop the habit of eating two meals per day.** This habit will cause a remarkable change in your system and constitution. And in addition, if you are selective and eat only sathwic food, you will create the right and proper vibrations for *dhyana* and *sadhana*.

S - When we talk about *sathwic* food, does it mean only the physical organic food that we eat?

SAI - No, there are other things too because there are other organs in the body. Apart from the mouth, there are the eyes, ears and hands.

If you take the ***mouth***, it is the cause of three things - taste, talk and temper. The tongue revels in sampling tasty food. It also revels in talk. Sometimes, it is led uncontrollably into uttering falsehood, loose-talk, gossip, backbiting and criticism. At times, the tongue wags furiously and lashes out in a temper. All these set off adverse vibrations in the body and mind. Physical and mental health get affected. There is no ease and no peace. So, it is very important to control the three T's - taste buds, talk and temper. The tongue should be trained and disciplined to eat only *sathwic* food, speak only the truth and forsake temper.

The *eyes* are the windows of the mind. Just as you keep the windows in your house shut against dust, smoke, rain or gale, your eyes should be closed to undesirable sights. See only the good and do not look at the bad. A rose is surrounded by thorns but you enjoy the beauty of the rose and do not even notice the thorns. The thorns prick and hurt but the rose only delights. Similarly, as you go through life, allow your eyes to dwell only on the good and the pleasant; ignore the bad and the unpleasant. Avoid all trashy films and vulgar novels. Let your eyes imbibe only what is good and what is *sathwic*.

The *ears* are the doors of the mind. Don't you keep the doors of your house shut against unwelcome visitors and thieves? Similarly, the ears should keep out the unwelcome visitors of gossip, scandal, falsehood and untruth. They are like thieves who invade the privacy of your home and steal your peace. Therefore, do not allow your ears to listen to loose and undesirable talk. Hear only good.

Next are the *hands*. They are the most important among the *Karmendriyas* (organs of action). The hands should be used only for doing good - for carrying out one's own duties with devotion and discipline, for helping those who are in need, for serving the poor and the destitute and for striving for the welfare of society. Never let your hands point fingers of criticism at others. Remember that when one finger is pointing at someone, three are pointing at you. Use your hands only as instruments of service. Service to mankind is service to God.

Therefore, speak good, see good, hear good, do good and be good - this is the way to God. In this manner, your mind will be cleansed and purified *Chitha suddhi* will help you to realize God.

S - Baba, please tell me something about fasting. Is it really necessary?

SAI - First, you have to be very clear about the real meaning of fasting. What do you do when you fast? You abstain or keep away from food. But, the tongue is not the only organ in the body. There are other organs like the eyes and ears. Keeping the eyes away from *rajasic* and *tamasic* sights; keeping the ears away from *rajasic* and *tamasic* talk - are these also not a way of fasting? Fasting does not mean starving the body of food. Fasting is abstinence. It means that one abstains from *unsathwic* food of any type, whether it is food that we imbibe through the mouth, eyes or ears. The real meaning of fasting is to control all the senses and see that they abstain and keep away from evil and undesirable things. It does not mean missing meals or not eating rice, as some people think.

The Sanskrit word for fasting is "*upavasa*". But there is a far deeper meaning attached to the word. "*Upa*" means near or close and "*vasa*" means to live or dwell. So, the word "*upavasa*" means to live near or to dwell close. Live near or dwell close to whom? To God, of course. The mind should be fixed unwaveringly on the Lord and in all moments of waking, eating, working and moving, the mind should cry, "God, God, God". That is true "*upavasa*". *Upavasa* is to constantly experience the presence of God and to develop a close and intimate relationship with Him. This is the real meaning of "*upavasa*", not missing out on meals and starving the stomach. People say, "Today is *Amavasya* (new-moon), so I will not eat", or "Today is *Pournami* (full-moon), so I will eat only after sighting the moon", and so on. They keep away from food but they do not keep their minds on God. All sorts of other things occupy their thoughts and minds. This is not "*upavasa*" in the true sense of the word. What is the use of abstaining from food when the mind is wandering everywhere except towards God?

If you want to practise "*upavasa*" sincerely, the way to do it is to control the senses, discipline the mind and keep it centered on God. Abstain from unnecessary desires, control your wants and keep a tight rein over your senses. The senses are like horses. Unless you keep a tight hold over them, they will stray here and there. Instal the *buddhi* (intelligence) as the *sarathi* (driver) and hold the reins firmly with a steady hand. Then you will be able to guide the senses along the right path. Once the senses are controlled, the desires also fade away and the mind becomes docile and calm. It is die-mind and becomes a diamond. Then your path is clear to perceive God. This is how "*upavasa*" should be observed and practised.

Notes:- *Some of the foods can be classified as follows:-

Rajasic - fish, eggs, meat, chillies, pickles, tamarind, mustard, sour things, hot things, tea, coffee, cocoa, white sugar, carrots, turnips, spices.

Tamasic - Beef, pork, wine, onions, garlic, tobacco, rotten things, stale things, unclean things, all intoxicants, all liquors, all drugs.

Sathwic - Cow's milk, cream, cheese, butter, curd, ghee, sweet fruits, vegetables, dried fruits and nuts, wheat, rice, barley, jaggery or brown sugar, green gram, Bengal gram, ginger, honey.

**Yogis usually eat only one solid meal at 12 noon everyday. Those who eat two meals a day normally take their food at 9.30 A.M. and 6.30 P.M.

THE DARK PERIOD

S - There are periods in my life when I feel that I have fallen and during these times, I am not able to carry on with my usual *sadhana* and *dhyana*. Why does this happen, Baba?

SAI - Every *sadhaka* goes through these periods, the so-called "dark periods". There are changes going on within you during these periods of which you are not aware. It is the period of maturity and at the end of it, you emerge a stronger and better person. It is like baking a Christmas Cake. You mix all the ingredients and bake them and then you put away the cake inside for a few days and allow it to mature and mellow. After that, it tastes richer and sweeter. Or, take a wine-maker for example. He makes the syrup from the grapes and stores it away inside for months. During this time, it ferments and bubbles and becomes a sweet wine. It is the same in the case of *sadhana* also. You are only going through a process of maturing. So, do not think that you have fallen in any way.

S - What exactly is this process of maturing, Baba? What does it mean?

SAI - During your *sadhana*, you would have undergone various experiences and learnt many things. All these facts have to be assimilated by the inner spirit, analysed and converted into knowledge and wisdom. Sometimes, this is done consciously by you yourself through the process of *"vichaara"* (inquiry) and *"viveka"* (discrimination). But at other times, this translation of experience into wisdom takes place without your awareness, in the dark. And therefore, the dark period.

For example, what happens after you have eaten a meal? The food has to be absorbed, digested and assimilated by the system. You cannot see the process of digestion and assimilation, but they go on in the body. It is the same in the case of spiritual food also. You read religious books, listen to *bhajans* and discourses, take part in *sathsang* sessions, practise *sadhana* and *dhyana*. All these are food for the spirit within. The spiritual food has to be absorbed, digested and assimilated by the inner self. The end result of this process is spiritual, mental and emotional growth and maturity.

S - Is it because these changes take place that we are sometimes caught up in a sort of spiritual inertia, Baba?

SAI - Yes. This maturing period is one of confusion to the *sadhaka*. You feel confused, bewildered, lost, like a rudderless ship floundering in the dark and trying desperately to reach the lighted shore.

S - Baba, at such times, I do not have the same feeling of closeness with you.

SAI - Yes, I know. You feel adrift. You do not have any spiritual well being. But this is only a temporary phase at the end of which, the inner self emerges purer, stronger and nobler. For example, if you have an illness, you do not have physical well-being. The doctor treats you for the illness by giving you medicines and tonics. You yourself cannot see the curing process that is effected by the medicines. But the curing is taking place within you. When the course of treatment is over, the body regains its normal health and well-being.

Similarly, when spiritual changes and transformations are taking place within, you are overcome by a feeling of mental and spiritual lassitude. But when the maturing process is over, the darkness is lifted, the day dawns and you come out into the light, a stronger and wiser person.

S - You are the *Sadguru*, Baba. Do you formulate and control the spiritual changes in us?

SAI - Yes, I monitor your spiritual growth and regulate your progress. I know your past and the degree of spiritual evolution you have achieved in past births. Based on your past development, I help you in your present *sadhana* and direct and control your spiritual growth. I know how much you progressed before and how much you must progress now. It is like making a sweet. The cook knows at which point the sugar syrup is of the right consistency, when to add the flour, when to add the ghee and the essence, how much to add and at which exact point the sweet is ready to be removed from the fire. Similarly, I mix and add and stir until you reach a certain degree of spiritual awareness.

S - How often do these phases of maturing occur in a sadhaka's life?

SAI - It depends on the level of the *sadhaka's* spiritual attainment. Unlike the growth of the physical body, spiritual growth has to be very slow and gradual. The growth is spread out over a series of births. But, if you take one single birth, there will be many phases, many dark periods. A sincere *sadhaka* has to necessarily go through quite a few periods of inner development. The frequency of occurrence of these periods depends on the spiritual fibre of the person, just as learning depends upon the I.Q. Some people can imbibe and absorb at a faster rate than others. But even those who are on a highly advanced plane of learning go through these periods at some points in their lives. Even the ancient *rishis* and *yogis* used to undergo them, although no one talked about them.

S - Approximately when in a *sadhaka's* life do these periods occur, Baba ?

SAI - Naturally, not in the very beginning. The earlier stages in the path of the *sadhaka* are all experiences, thrills and ecstasies. It is only after some time that the inner self begins to evolve. The changes begin to take place, say at the middle of the path. It is then that the real process of learning starts.

Think of a *sadhaka's* progress as climbing a mountain. You climb enthusiastically for some little height. Then you are tired and when you reach a ledge or small plateau, you stop and take rest. After some time, you recover your breath, re-coup your strength and are ready to resume your climbing. Thus, you keep climbing and resting until you reach the peak of the mountain.

The periods of maturing in a sadhaka's life are similar to the plateaus. When the darkness lifts and light breaks, you will emerge re-vitalised and re-invigorated, ready to move to greater heights. So, do not get disheartened or dejected when you are caught in this phase. It is the time of shaping, moulding and polishing. It is the time when real development and evolution take place within.

S - What do You advise us to do during such times, Baba?

SAI - It is the time for more karma and seva. This leads to "*trikarana suddhi*" - the purification of the three instruments: the hands, the tongue and the mind. When you are engaged in karma and seva, the hands and tongue are occupied and kept busy and do not give way to the attendant vices. When these two are purified, the mind also becomes pure and cool like the moon. Thus, you can combine external purification with the internal which is taking place within you.

S - Will this help us to come out of the dark period faster?

SAI - Yes, if you recognise the period for what it is. You can help speed up the internal development by adopting the correct external practices. If you are able to combine the two, you will help spiritual growth. And when the period of evolution is over, your inner self will emerge with new energy, vigour and vitality, ready to engage in fresh sadhana and move to higher planes of experiences and learning.

MAYA, MITHYA AND NITHYA

SAI - Today, I'll tell you what is meant by Maya, Mithya and Nithya. Before creation, there was only Brahman or Chaitanya or Super-consciousness. There was only the existence of pure knowledge. But what is the use of pure knowledge without Its external manifestation and outward form? What is the use of a seed without a flower, of a flower without a fruit? And so, the idea of creation was born. The Super-consciousness or Brahman donned the vesture of Maya from which came the force called Maya Shakti. From this *Shakti* came the three *Gunas* (*rajas*, *tamas* and *sathwa*) and out of permutations and combinations of these *Gunas*, emerged the *Panchabhuthas* (the five elements of earth, water, fire, wind and sky) and the *Indriyas* (the senses).

S - One moment please, Baba. When we normally speak of Maya we take it to mean illusion and delusion. Isn't that what You are talking about?

SAI - What is Maya? It means invisible, something which is unseen. When you refer to Maya in terms of illusion, you understand it as something intangible. But Maya has a force which is tangible. Otherwise, how can it function?

If you take the wind, for example, you cannot see it but you feel its force, power and energy when it blows. So, the wind is intangible but it has a force which is tangible. The two cannot be separate, they are co-existent. It is the same in the case of Maya also. In the narrower sense, it means illusion. But it also possesses Shakti (force or energy) and the two are synonymous, just as wind and its force are synonymous. You say "the wind is blowing" or "the wind is strong". You don't say "the wind-force is blowing" or "the wind-force is strong". Similarly, Maya and Maya-Shakti are one and the same.

S - When we talk of Maya and Maya-Shakti, are we actually referring to the primeval Shakti, the Cosmic Energy?

SAI - Yes, both are the same. Maya Shakti means the unseen invisible force. This Shakti is the subtlest form of energy and is the root of all creation. It is the Primordial, Cosmic, Universal Energy.

S - Is this the *Shiva-Shakti* aspect?

SAI - Yes, Chaitanya or Super-Consciousness is *Shiva*. The active force behind creation is *Shakti*.

S - And what is meant by Purusha and Prakriti?

SAI - They refer to individual consciousness and individual energy. The Shiva-Shakti aspect is present in each and every part of creation as Purusha-Prakriti. Purusha is the male aspect and represents consciousness or knowledge. Prakriti is the female aspect and represents energy. The Shiva-Shakti element is macro-cosmic while the Purusha-Prakriti element is micro-cosmic. Both emanate from the same source namely Brahman. What is present in man is micro-cosmic force (Purusha - Prakriti) which is a part of the macro-cosmic force (Shiva-Shakti).

S - It is all quite clear now, Baba.

SAI - Good. Now, as I said earlier, it is Maya which gave rise to creation. When I say "Maya", I mean "Maya-Shakti", of course, for the two are synonymous. It is Maya which is behind the entire created universe. Maya is the cause, creation is the effect. All the things you see around you - the mineral, plant and animal kingdoms, man and everything else existent in the universe have their source in Maya. From Maya they come and into Maya they go, for all created things are subject to decay, destruction and death.

And now, you must listen carefully and understand. All you see around you- the plants, birds, animals, earth, water, mountains, even human beings - seem to be real, do they not? You can see them, touch them, feel them, smell them and hear them, so they all seem to be very real to you. But they are not real. They are only apparently and seemingly real. They are Mithya. Mithya means that which is transient, temporary, mutable, not permanent. How can something which does not last be considered real? So, the entire creation itself is unreal, Mithya, since it is bound by the laws of dissolution, decay and death.

Here, you must have a clear idea of the difference between Maya and Mithya. For example, if you take a tree, it is subject to decay; so, it is not lasting and therefore it is Mithya. But the energy or force which gave "life" to the tree is lasting and this is Maya.

S - What you say then, Baba, is that the life-force pervading the entire universe is always permanent and therefore real and this is Maya. All else is Mithya.

SAI - Yes, like the yarn and the cloth. You can see the cloth but not the yarn from which it came. Can there be cloth without yarn? The yarn is Maya and the cloth is Mithya. I shall give you some more examples to illustrate the difference.

Take the case of a mirage in the desert. The mirage is produced by a play of light and certain desert conditions. When viewed from a distance, it looks as if there is a lake or a pool of water. But, when you go nearer, you find nothing. The water seems real but is not and therefore it is Mithya. The sun or the light from the sun which caused the mirage is Maya.

And now, we come to the third factor - Nithya. Nithya means eternal, immutable, permanent and everlasting. It is something which is even subtler than Maya.

S - Does it refer to Chaitanya or Pure Consciousness, Baba?

SAI - Yes. While Maya constantly moves and changes, Nithya is ever still and motionless. In the example of the mirage, we have seen that the water is Mithya and the sun is Maya. But that which lights up the sun or gives light to the sun - that is Nithya, Eternal, Absolute. This "thing" or "being" which is Nithya has been given various names like Brahman, Chaitanya, Hiranya-Garbha and so on.

I'll give you another example. You sit in the theatre with the screen in front of you. The light is switched on and various characters are projected through it on to the screen. You watch the play of figures on the screen. They move, they talk, the screen comes alive and seems very real to you. But when the film show is over, what happens to these characters? They just disappear. It is as if they have never been. So, these characters are Mithya. The light which projected them on the screen and caused the figures to be seen is Maya. And, the current in the light or bulb is Nithya.

Or take the case of an actor on the stage. The actor puts on a disguise and adopts certain mannerisms and characteristics. With the help of these aids, he projects another and totally different personality to the audience. He creates a new person altogether. This new personality presented to the audience is *Mithya*. The disguise with all its appendages is *Maya*. The actor is *Nithya*. Once the disguise is removed, what happens? Everything crumbles, only *Nithya* remains.

Again, we have the traditional example of the rope and the snake. You see a rope in the dark and think it is a snake. But when light comes, you realize your mistake and discover that it is only a rope. *Maya*, first as darkness and then as light, caused the same object to appear as two different things. The rope is *Mithya*, the darkness and light are *Maya* and that which caused *Maya* is *Nithya*.

S - Yes, it is quite clear now, Baba. Knowing these distinctions will help to lift the veil of ignorance, won't it?

SAI - Yes, Avidya will disappear when you realize what lies behind the apparent and the seeming. For instance, you will look at a tree and know that it is God's handiwork. You will perceive its dignity, stateliness and gracefulness and recognise the force which gave shape and life to it. And you will look at it and love it, not for what it merely is but also for what you see in it - that is, God. Whether it is a beautiful plant, a delicate flower, a pretty bird, a colourful landscape, a golden sunrise or a silvery moon, you will realize that they are all reflections of God. You begin to see His Hand in everything. And you will grow to love Nature not merely for what it is, but for what it depicts.

Nature is very close to God, closer than man is, for in man there is a veil of ignorance clouding his vision and marring his sight. But Nature is the purest handiwork of God. If you are able to love Nature and feel in tune with it, you are that much closer to God. It is very easy to know God through Nature, for in Nature there is goodness, simplicity, purity and selflessness.

S - You often say that there are many lessons to be learnt from Nature.

SAI - That is right. Nature is the best teacher. A tree gives shade to others and takes nothing for itself. It gives fruits to others but does not itself partake of them. A plant sprouts beautiful flowers and gives joy to others but does not enjoy the beauty by itself. The sun is constantly at work, giving life, light and energy to the world. Does it ask for anything in return? No, it performs Nishkamya Karma, that is action without the desire for reward. These are some examples of the selfless Nature and are perfect lessons to the selfishness of man. If only man watches and studies Nature carefully, he can imbibe a lot of philosophy from it, which will help to make him a better person. Nature is an ideal Guru and if you treat it as such and develop love and reverence towards it, you will move closer to God.

S - But Baba, there is so much ugliness in Nature. There are ugly creatures, for instance, and one finds it difficult to appreciate their existence.

SAI - Now, here we come to the question of duality and non-duality- Dwaita and Adwaita. It is true that there is ugliness in Nature and in all creation, but everything has its place and purpose. Nothing was created without a reason. What is ugliness, after all! It is the other side of beauty. Beauty and Ugliness, to use an English phrase are two sides of the same coin opposite ends of the same stick. Thus, we have two sides to every aspect - good and bad, beauty and ugliness, truth and untruth, light and darkness, knowledge and ignorance, and so on. They are complementary; where one exists, the other also does. Can you appreciate beauty unless you know what ugliness is? Can you be good unless you know what is bad? Can you practise truth unless you know what is untruth? Can you recognise light unless you know what is darkness? This is the duality aspect - Dwaita.

Actually, what appears as dual is one. Both emanate from the One Supreme Force. It is like the illusion of the rope and the snake. When you recognise this with the help of inner vision, you realize that all this is Adwaita, non-dual, One.

S - Baba, it is easy to perceive God in goodness and beauty but difficult to do so in badness and ugliness.

SAI - Ah, there you have avidya clouding your vision. You are referring to two different things - physical sight and mental vision. This is where viveka or discrimination has to come in. Things like ugliness and badness do not appear pleasant to the physical senses. You see and judge the things around you with your outer sensory organs. But in order to see what lies behind and beneath, you have to develop inner perception or mental vision. You must learn to discriminate between Maya and Mithya and this will help you to perceive God in everything. In this way, you will develop a feeling of closeness to Nature and to God and an awareness of oneness.

You must cultivate this feeling of oneness with the help of discrimination, inquiry and sadhana. Then, this awareness will grow within you and you will be able to perceive the quality of the oneness of everything. You will find yourself moving closer to an understanding of the Supreme and Absolute Consciousness.

THE KINSHIP OF LOVE

S - Baba, you were explaining the difference between Maya, Mithya and Nithya. How would You explain these with respect to man?

SAI - Yes, this is the most important part to be understood. You know that the make-up of a human personality is complex. The original seed of divinity is buried deep and hidden under five layers or sheaths called *panchakosas**. These obscure the inner vision and prevent man from realizing his latent divinity. The panchakosas are the body, senses, mind, intellect and bliss. All these are mithya because they are not permanent. The body is subject to death. The senses exist and function in relation to the objective world. They produce desires, impulses, feelings, emotions, etc. which go collectively to form the mind. Based on the desires and impulses, the mind builds an image or a picture of oneself which forms the ego. Thus the mind and the ego depend upon the senses for their existence. They feed continuously on the sensations produced by the senses.

For example, if you take water, it has no definite form or shape of its own. It merely takes on the shape of the container or vessel into which it is poured. Similarly, the mind by itself has no form. It exists because the senses are functioning. Once the senses are withdrawn from the external objects, all desires and impulses fade away, dissolving the mind and the ego with it. So, you see that these three - the senses, mind and ego - are subject to dissolution and do not last and therefore they are *Mithya*.

As for the intellect, it is the purest among the *kosas* or sheaths because it functions separately, on its own, independent of the working of the others. It is not affected by external agencies. The intellect is rational, discriminating and analytical. It is never swayed by bias or prejudice and therefore it is never wrong in its dictates. Unfortunately, the human tendency is such that the intellect is more often than not obscured and clouded by the mind and its vagaries. The judgement of the intellect is always pure but the mind intervenes and interprets in its own way, according to its raga - dweshas (likes and dislikes). Now, this intellect also is not permanent. At a certain point in the path of *self-realization*, the intellect is to be discarded or shed like the other sheaths. At this point, awareness exists on a level beyond the intelligence. So, the intellect too can be regarded as *Mithya*.

The last of the five sheaths is that of Bliss and it comprises of ignorance. It is the deep-sleep state of consciousness which is considered blissful because all sensations, feelings and agitations are stilled in this state. But even this sheath does not remain once *self-realization* is attained. So, this too is *Mithya*. All the panchakosas are shed as knowledge progresses.

S - Baba, Is it right to say that a man functions at the level of pure consciousness when the panchakosas are shed?

SAI - Yes. Once you transcend the intelligence you reach another level, namely the intuition. The intuition is directly attuned to *Chith* (Consciousness). The intuitive force is derived from *Chith*. So, you can think of intuition as *Maya Shakti*.

S - Is it the same as conscience?

SAI - No. Conscience is the voice of the intellect. Intuition is the voice of God, the Inner Voice. While conscience tells you what is right and what is wrong, intuition tells you what "is" and what "is not". Ideally, man should function at the intuitive level but it takes years of sadhana and self-discipline to achieve this.

S - Is that the state of pure consciousness?

SAI - Yes. But there is another state beyond this called the Super-Consciousness. This is *Chith* or *Chaitanya* or *Brahman*. It is eternal, immutable and indestructible and so it is *Nithya*. In micro-cosmic terms, it is called *Purusha* and the corresponding energy or life-force is called *Prakriti*. These two, *Purusha* and *Prakriti* (*Nithya* and *Maya*) are present as common factors in every man and being. It is only the other *kosas* or sheaths which are different. The external structure may be different but the inner core is the same. For example, you can make sweets of different types, sizes and shapes with sugar, flour and ghee. Though the outer forms are different, the essential sweetness is basically the same. If you recognise this in relation to the people around you, you will be a step nearer towards realizing the Truth.

S - You mean the oneness and unity of all mankind and creation.

SAI - Yes. But what is more important is that all mankind and everything in the universe are bound together by the same bond and that is *Love*. The entire creation is a kinship of love. What is God? What is Energy? What is Consciousness? They are nothing but Love. God is Love. It is the power of love alone that binds all humanity alike. It is this intangible force that forges the unity of all creation. If you are able to feel this love, then you have realized the Highest Truth.

S - I am ashamed to say it, Baba, but some people have such unattractive qualities and unlovable natures that they fail to inspire love. It is easier to turn away from them. I know it is wrong but how should we overcome this failing?

SAI - Yes, it is a common human failing. First, you should understand that though the exterior may be harsh, rough and prickly, the interior is sweet. A jackfruit or a pineapple is prickly outside but sweet inside. As I told you before, the outer forms vary but the inner core of all mankind is the same, saturated with the sweetness of love and divinity. It is up to you to try and see beneath the external appearance and reach below the surface.

Take diamonds, for example. Some are buried very deep under many layers of dust, mud and soil while some others are found fairly close to the surface. The ones that are buried deep will have more coatings of mud and dirt and will have a more rough exterior than the others, and to all outward appearances will look like ordinary stones. But the expert does not discard them as useless. He carefully scrapes away the layers of mud and cleans up the dirt, until the pure fineness and luster of the gem are revealed. Similarly, the latent divinity and purity of man are buried under layers of avidya (ignorance). It is ignorance which is responsible for man's baser qualities and traits. The true and essential nature of man is sweetness. Love is his natural state. But years and years of ignorance have obscured his vision and hidden his true self from himself. He identifies himself with the body and the senses, interacts with the objective world and acts and behaves accordingly. But, a person with discrimination and perception learns to look below the outer surface and tries to see God in himself and in others as well.

S - It is difficult to do so in actual life, Baba, especially when people's attitudes and behaviour are negative.

SAI - Then, `you' should be positive. You must cultivate love towards everyone, regardless of what they are like or what they do. You have no right to judge whether a person is good or bad, or whether an action of his is good or bad. Leave the judgement to God. He is the only Judge of persons, things and actions. What you have to do is to offer love to others. However hateful or unendearing a person may be, you must show love, affection, understanding, tolerance, sympathy, charity and compassion. All these are sathwic qualities; Godly qualities. It is the only way. Love is the only remedy, the only cure for any human malady. It is the only way in which you will get a positive and favourable response.

For how long can a person hold out against love? For how long can he remain unaffected by its softness and sweetness? Sooner or later he will succumb to it. How can he reject that which is his true, intrinsic nature? Does one reject happiness and joy? No, because happiness is the natural state and unhappiness is the unnatural state. So also, love is the natural state and all other contrary emotions are unnatural. Therefore, when you send a wave of spontaneous love to a person, it is bound to strike some chord in him or her. When you go on showering love, it will slowly begin to cleanse and purify, and soon the undesirable traits will be weeded out and goodness will shine through.

Love is the only alchemy, the only solution in the *Kali Yuga*. It is the only possible weapon with which to fight the evil tendencies. One should not meet hate with hate. One should meet hate with love. I tell you, love is the most wonderful thing and can work great miracles by changing the very nature and character of man. It works from within the person, from inside, and so the change is more thorough and absolute, though the curing process is slow. Therefore, develop love towards everyone. You must try and see only the goodness in them. No one can be completely bad. There will be at least one redeeming quality in him and that is enough to start with. Hold on to that and ignore the baser qualities. Don't look for the bad, look only for the good. See good, be good and do good. Give them love without any desire for return or reward. Then you will surely realize God.

Note:- *Panchakosas are the five sheaths or concentric layers of matter enveloping the *Atma*. They have no separate existence as such but are so analysed only for purposes of study. The five sheaths are as follows :-

1. Annamaya Kosa or the Food Sheath which comprises of the gross physical body, the five sense organs (the eyes, ears, nose, tongue and skin) and the five organs of action (the vocal organs, hands, feet, genital organs and excretory organs).

2. Pranamaya Kosa or the Vital Air Sheath which comprises of the five senses (form, sound, smell, taste and touch) and the five physiological systems (the faculties of perception, excretion, digestion, circulation and thinking).

3. Manomaya Kosa or The Mental Sheath which comprises of the mind and the ego.

4. Vignanamaya Kosa or The Intellectual Sheath which comprises of the intelligence.

5. Anandamaya Kosa or The Bliss Sheath which comprises ignorance, non-apprehension and the state of deep sleep.

The *Atma* is the core of this five-sheathed structure. The five sheaths are like five layers of cloth worn by a person, but which are totally different from the wearer. So too, the *Atma* is distinct and separate from the five sheaths.

INCARNATION OF GOD

S - Baba, why does God always incarnate as a man?

SAI - Brahman, the Supreme Absolute Consciousness is Formless; it is neither man nor woman, male nor female. But when the Consciousness splits, it takes on two aspects - Knowledge and *Energy, Shiva* and *Shakti. Shiva* is the male or the negative aspect while *Shakti* is the female or the positive aspect. *Shiva* and *Shakti* are immanent everywhere as *Purusha* and Prakriti respectively. *Purusha* represents the innate consciousness while *Prakriti* represents all creation including mankind. As I said, *Shiva* or *Purusha* is the male aspect and *Shakti* or Prakriti is the female aspect. God is the only *Purusha* or male in creation. All else and everything else is female. That is why God always takes a male form when He incarnates on earth.

S - Why have all the incarnations been in India?

SAI - Because India is the land of the *Vedas* and of Hinduism. The Vedas are the Voice of God and Hinduism is the oldest religion in the world. All the other religions came from Hinduism. So India is the birthplace of all religions. All the major religions of the world are represented collectively in India. That is why God always incarnates here, to demonstrate the unity of all religions and faiths and to establish a common brotherhood of man and Fatherhood of God.

S - In one of Your discourses, You stated that Shiva and *Shakti* had promised the sage Bharadwaja that They would incarnate thrice in his lineage - Shiva as Shirdi Sai, Shiva and

Shakti as Sathya Sai and *Shakti* as Prema Sai. What is the basis for such a distinction, Baba?

SAI - It is a question of *Shakti* - manifestation. Shirdi Sai was a Brahma Jnani. He was the Embodiment of Universal Consciousness - Jnanaswaroopa. He was also the Sadguru teaching His devotees the Reality and guiding them along the path of Truth.

S - Then, was He not a *Poorna-Avatar*?*

SAI - Oh yes, He was a *Poorna-Avatar* and possessed all the attributes of a *Poorna Avatar*. But He did not manifest His *Shakti* or Power freely. He had all the attributes of Divine *Shakti* but He held them in check and did not reveal them fully. He was like a learned musician who exhibited his musical skills occasionally; He was like a gifted poet who gave voice to his verse only rarely; He was like a skilled sculptor who revealed his artistry sometimes.

S - Yet, He is known to have manifested His *Shakti* and performed miracles as You do, Baba. He even revived the dead.

SAI - Yes, but these Divine siddhis (miracles) and leelas (sport) were merely outpourings of love for His devotees. They were not meant to attract but only to safe-guard and protect. He did not use them like visiting-cards. He used His *Shakti* only to save His devotees from distress and trouble, from sorrow and pain. He performed so-called miracles, not for their own sake but as a means of protecting the devotees from harm and danger. But even so, the full potential of His

Divine Shakti was not revealed. It was not really necessary for Him to perform miracles in order to attract.

S - Why was that, Baba?

SAI - Because people in those days had simple faith and belief. They had the ability to recognise a saint or an *Avatar* through their own perception and wisdom. They did not need proof of greatness or divinity. They accepted divinity because of their simple devotion. They were attracted to Shirdi Sai by His Swabhava (Nature) and not by His acts. They looked upon Him and served Him as the Great Teacher, the Divine Sadguru.

Unfortunately, the nature of people's belief and faith has changed in these days. They have forgotten what is simplicity of thought, values and beliefs. They pay attention only to something which is unusual, sensational, extraordinary and miraculous.

S - Hence your visiting-cards !

SAI - Yes, I use My *Shakti* to attract people to draw them towards the Godward path. These miracles are merely baits with which I lure them towards Me. Once their faith is firmly established, they begin to look beyond the miracles and slowly start stretching their hands out for what I have really come to give - Knowledge and Bliss.

This Sathya Sai Incarnation is one where you see the full manifestation and exercise of all the sixteen attributes of a Poorna Avatar. I am the Embodiment of *Shiva* and *Shakti*, that is Universal Consciousness and Universal Energy. And I show evidences of both to the fullest extent.

S - Yes Baba, Your devotees have all experienced your Divinity a number of times and in many ways. Will Your Incarnation as Prema Sai be a continuation of what You have started now?

SAI - Yes. Prema Sai will be *Shakti* incarnate. He will work ceaselessly for the good of the world and will establish love, goodwill and peace. His Name and Fame will reach every corner of the earth. He will be the Universal Guru, the World Teacher, a Leader of leaders. In the *Dwapara Yuga*, Krishna was Advisor and Friend to the Pandavas. He instructed and guided them in the ruling of the kingdom and taught His devotees the truth of His Divinity. The function of Prema Sai will be the same. His Voice will be heard all over the world. He will receive universal recognition and devotion and will directly lead the world towards truth, love and peace.

S - Baba, what will be the position of India then?

SAI - India will be the leader of the world in all respects - spiritually, culturally, socially, politically and economically. All her past glory, culture and traditions will be revived and she will shine forth as the leading nation of the world. This is how it was *yugas* ago and this is how it will be once more.

Note:- A Poorna Avatar (Full Incarnation) is said to possess sixteen *kalas* or attributes. The five main attributes are :-

1. *Srishti* or the power of creation.
2. *Sthithi* or the power of preservation.
3. *Laya* or the power of dissolution.
4. *Tilodayak* or the power to incarnate.
5. *Anugraha* or the power to shower Grace.

Each of these five attributes are present in all the three Time-periods (Past, Present and Future) making the total number of attributes fifteen (5 x 3). The sixteenth attribute is *Chith* which means Consciousness or Awareness and this is present through all the ages of Time.

Among all the *Avatars*, only Sri Krishna and Sri Sai are said to be *Poorna Avatars*, possessing all the sixteen attributes. Even Sri Rama possessed only twelve attributes. The four remaining attributes were shared by Sri Parasurama and by Rama's three brothers - Lakshmana, Shatrughna and Bharatha - who possessed one attribute each.

KARMA AND THE CYCLE
OF BIRTH-DEATH

S- We know that *karma* and birth are directly linked and that one's birth is determined by one's *karma*. There are some questions that I would like to ask You on this subject, Baba.

SAI - Yes, yes. But you must understand one thing clearly at the outset. When you talk of *karma* in the context of birth and rebirth, you must know that the term "*karma*" does not mean only action. When there is an action, there is always a reaction. So, *karma* with respect to birth and rebirth refers to the chain of action and reaction. Is it clear to you?

S - Not quite, Baba. When you speak of "reaction", do you mean the result proceeding from the action? The fruit of action?

SAI - No, that is not what I mean. Naturally every action will have a result and the type of result depends on the type of action. As you sow, so shall you reap. Action - result, performance - consequence; the two are bound up together and cannot be separated. But when I talk of "reaction", I do not mean the result of action. What I mean is your reaction to the result; the response or the manner in which you receive the fruit of action. It is important for you to understand this because it is not action itself which causes rebirth but the reaction.

S - Do you mean our attitude towards the fruit of action, Baba?

SAI - Yes, I mean your attitude and the way in which you receive the fruit or the result of your action. You feel happy and elated when the result is good; you feel unhappy and dejected when the result is bad. These emotional responses set off further desires and impulses which inflate or deflate the ego. This in turn leads to more action, and action results in reaction and thus a never-ending chain of action - reaction - rebirth is produced. The desires and impulses remain with you even after death. They are so strong that you are born into this world again and again in order to fulfil them. As long as desires remain, re-birth is unavoidable. So, if you wish to avoid re-birth, you should get rid of worldly desires. They are binding on you. They are like magnets which attract you again and again into this world. Therefore, if you wish to escape from the cycle of birth and death and re-birth, you should try to give up desires. Since desires are caused by your emotional responses, you should try to change your attitude towards the result or fruit of action.

S - How should we go about this task, Baba?

SAI - Well, my dear, the attitudes of elation and dejection, happiness and unhappiness towards the fruit of action exist because you think that you are the "doer" of actions and the "enjoyer" of fruits. As long as this idea exists, you will be bound by the cycle of birth and re-birth. But once you realize that you are only a silent witness and an onlooker, you will be freed from the cycle.

S - We can say that this attitude of happiness towards success and unhappiness towards failure arises because we identify ourselves with the body and not with the *Atma*. Isn't it so, Baba?

SAI - Yes. You think that you are the body, the mind, the intellect and so on. That is why you react emotionally to the consequences of action. You think that the body "does" and the body "enjoys". But who are you really? You are not the body. You are something different and separate from the mere body, unaffected by any action or result. You, the essential you, are the *Atma*. You are only a witness to what is going on around you, for the *Atma* does not engage in action. Whatever is taking place does not affect the real "You".

S - If I am only the witness, who then is the real "doer" and "enjoyer"?

SAI - God is the only "Doer" of all acts and He is the only "Enjoyer" of all fruits. He is the only *Kartha* and *Bhoktha*. All acts are done by Him and all fruits go to Him. He is present everywhere and in everything as *Atma*. The *Atma* is the source of all action just as the current is the source of light. You are only instruments in the hands of *Atma* or God. Here, when I say "You", I do not mean the real you (*Atma*) but your physical body. Your body, mind, intellect and ego are like instruments in God's Hands and through them He performs acts. In order to write, you need a paper and pen, do you not? Similarly, God acts through you. And since He performs the actions, only He is entitled to enjoy the fruits of the actions.

I will give you an example. Take a puppet show, for instance. The puppeteer has the dolls attached to strings. He jerks and pulls the strings and makes the dolls move and dance according to his wishes. The puppets cannot move of their own accord and will. They are entirely in the hands of the puppeteer. If the show is good, the puppeteer earns credit and if the show is bad, he earns discredit. So, you see, success or failure both belong to the puppeteer. He is the "doer" and he is the "enjoyer". The puppets are mere tools in his hands. It is the same in the case of God also. He is the Divine Puppeteer; He is the Doer and the Enjoyer. You are merely His dolls and tools.

Or, take another example a game of chess, for another example. The Grand-masters sit over the chessboard and move the chess coins around as they think fit. The success or failure accrues to the masters and not to the coins. The winner gets the credit and the loser gets the discredit. In either case, it is not the coins which enjoy the result.

So, you see that God is the Ultimate Doer, Giver and Receiver. He is the Kartha, *Datha* and *Bhoktha*. All actions are His, the fruits come from Him and they go back to Him. You are only instruments in His Hands and are witnesses. Therefore, since you are not the actual doer, you have no right over the fruits.

S - Just a minute, Baba. You say that we have no right over the fruits of action since God is the actual Doer. That's fair enough. But what about the action itself. Have we no right over action?

SAI - You have the right to exercise choice over action, whether or not a certain course of action has to be adopted. You have the right to choose between alternative courses of action. The courses or the paths leading to action are optional and are open to you. The action itself is predetermined and fixed, but the way in which it is done is left to your choice or preference. With the help of your intelligence and discrimination, you choose a certain course of action and execute it. This is where your right ends. Once the action is performed, the result or fruit passes out of your hands.

For example, suppose a man is seated in a car which is being driven by his chauffeur. The master tells the driver to go to a particular destination but leaves the choice of the route to him. The driver chooses the shortest and easiest path to reach the destination. The destination is fixed or pre-determined, only the alternative routes are open to choice. In other words, the action is fixed or pre-determined but the course of action is open to choice. Choosing the course of action from among alternatives is your right. But once you choose a certain course or path and the action or deed is done, the result passes out of your hands. The Law of *Karma* takes over and decides the result or the fruit of action. In the example of the car, the driver chooses a particular route and takes his master to his destination. With that, his action is over and his role or part is over. What happens after the destination is reached, what is got out of it, whether good or bad, success or failure does not concern him. He has no right to claim the result. The fruit or the result goes to the master. The master is the "enjoyer", the driver is only an instrument, a means to the end.

Similarly, your physical body, mind and intellect are instruments in God's Hands. He uses them to perform actions. You are like the driver and God is like the master. He is the actual Doer; you participate as a tool or observer and the fruits accrue to Him. Thus you see that God "does" and God "enjoys".

S - If you say that God does everything, then what about all the evil in the world, Baba? Surely God does not perform evil?

SAI - No, God does not by Himself perform evil. He prompts you and tells you to do only good. But what if you do not obey and carry out His instructions? The mind and the

ଓଃ 48 ଞ

ego are a bundle of desires, of *ragas* and dweshas (likes and dislikes) and they stand in the way of right action. It is like the mother telling the child to study, but the child in a mood of mischief goes out to play. The child disobeys the mother. The wrong is done by the child and not by the mother. Similarly, the Voice of God in you and your conscience may command you to do a certain thing, but the mind ignores the command and makes you do what it wants to do. So, it is not God who performs evil. It is your own mind and ego.

Man is blessed with the power of reasoning and the ability to discriminate between right and wrong. This is the function of the intellect - to discriminate, reason and analyse. The intellect tells you the correct thing to do. The intellect is always right. Unfortunately man does not listen to the intellect but only to the mind. As long as he does that, he will not do the correct thing.

S - Then, if everyone learns to follow only the intellect, no one will do any evil. Isn't it so, Baba?

SAI - Yes. The intellect is always right, unbiased, unprejudiced, balanced and rational. If you follow it, you are safe. You will not do or speak or think evil. Everything will be only good.

S - How are we to arrive at this state of thinking?

SAI - By constant vichaara and viveka - inquiry and discrimination. This will help you to realize that it is God who is the Doer and Enjoyer. He performs the action and He consumes the result. All acts come from Him and all fruits go to Him. When you begin to reason thus, you will automatically do only what is good and what is right, because in your reasoning God cannot do bad or wrong. You will follow only your intellect and not your mind.

S - Will we succeed in developing detachment, then, Baba?

SAI - Once you realize that you are not the "doer" and the "enjoyer", you will learn to renounce all rights over the fruits. You will not lay claim to the results of actions. You offer everything to the Lord. You surrender the act and the result to Him, as belonging only to Him. You cease to claim ownership or right over action and fruit. You become a *vairagin* or one who is detached. You become indifferent to the consequences of your action. Whether the result is good or bad, success or failure, you remain calm and unruffled, detached and unaffected.

S - Is this nishkamya *karma*, Baba?

SAI - Yes, it is. It is *karma* or action without desire for the fruit or reward. You will undertake every act only for its own sake and not for the sake of reward. The end result does not bother you. In this way, you become a *Karma-phala-thyagi*, that is, one who renounces the fruits of action.

S - Will *karma - phala - thyaga* liberate us from the cycle of birth and death?

SAI - Yes. You will become a *jeevan-mukta*, that is one who is liberated from the bondage of birth-death-rebirth while still living. There will be no more births for you. You will attain a state of equanimity and tranquillity. You will be in a constant state of peace which will not be shaken either by prosperity or by adversity. This is the perfect blissful state for which everyone should strive.

KARMIC LAW AND REBIRTH

S - May I ask you a few questions about *Karmic* Law and re-birth Baba?

SAI - Yes, But before you proceed, you should be clear on the point of *Karmic* Law. The Law of *Karma* is based purely on action. Every action has an equal and opposite reaction, resound and reflection. It is only this which is the basis for Karmic Law. You reap what you sow either in the same birth or in a succeeding birth. When you die, you carry with you not your worldly possessions, assets, name and fame, but only your deeds and misdeeds into the other world. When you are born into this world, you are born only with the garland of your deeds around your neck (*Karma* - kantamala).

Now, listen carefully. The *karma* of action and reaction determines whether or not you will have rebirth. (Here, reaction refers to your attitude towards the fruits of action). The Law of *Karma* based on action and result, performance and consequence, determines when, where, how and why you will have re-birth.

S - It is quite clear to me now, Baba. On this basis, I have a few questions to ask. First, why is a certain person born to certain parents?

SAI - *Karmic* debt is the reason for that. Your actions and *samskaras* make you beholden to certain people. You are indebted to them and this debt has to be repaid at sometime or the other. The debt need not be merely financial. It could be that you did something to a certain person or he did something to you. The damage has to be repaired and the debt has to be cancelled. If it is left unrepaired or uncancelled in this birth, it has to be set right in the next. This is what is meant by karmic debt. It is the main factor which decides why, where, when and how you will be re-born.

In the case of a certain person being born to certain parents, Karmic debt can work in three ways - the child has a karmic debt owing towards the parents, the parents have a karmic debt towards the child; or a mutual karmic debt exists between the parents and child which has to be repaid.

S - Does spiritual development determine the birth, Baba?

SAI - Yes, that is also a factor. A person who is spiritually evolved will take birth in a family which is pious and religious, and where the environment will be conducive to further spiritual growth. The family may be materially poor but spiritually it will be rich. Saint Thyagaraja, for example, was born into a poor but religious family.

S - How was it then that Prahlada was born of an asuric father?

SAI - That was a rare exception. But although Prahlada was born of an *asuric* (demonic) father, his guru brought him up with the name of God on his lips. Actually, Prahlada was born in order that Hiranyakasipu be taught a lesson. He met his end at the hands of Vishnu Himself.

S - Are all our present relationships due to past *karmic* actions and *karmic* debts?

SAI - All the important relationships like parent-child, husband-wife, brother-sister and guru-sishya are determined by past *karma*.

S - Does the parents' *karma* determine the type of children who will be born to them?

SAI - Yes. If the parents have good *karma*, they will be happy in their children, without worry, anxiety, etc. otherwise they will suffer through the bad fate or conduct of the children. Because of their past *karma*, they are fated to undergo this type of suffering. For example, Gandhari was a very pure and chaste woman but her *karma* caused her to suffer mental agony on account of her son's misdeeds.

S - Does the parents' *karma* affect the children, Baba?

SAI - No. The actions or deeds of the parents in a particular birth will affect the children in the same birth only. The effect will not be carried over to the next birth. For example, a father may incur heavy financial debts but dies before he is able to repay them. The burden of repaying the debts falls upon the son. The son is thus affected by his father's action in that birth only. The debt will be repaid in the same birth and will not be carried over to the next.

The parents' *karma* of past births does not affect the children. Everyone is born according to his or her own individual *karma*. When you die, you carry with you only your own good deeds and bad deeds, not other people's. When you are born, you have your own *karma-kantamala* around your neck and not other people's. So, one's present situation in life depends upon one's own *karma* or actions in the past and not on the *karma* of other people.

But although the parents' *karma* does not affect the *karma* of the children, both their *karmas* are related and inter-woven.

For example, suppose you have a set of parents who are good and noble in every way but they have an invalid child who is bed-ridden. Due to past *karma*, the parents are fated to undergo the sorrow of having an invalid child. The child, on account of past *karma*, is fated to undergo physical suffering. Or, suppose you have another set of parents who are also good and noble but are unhappy because their daughter is widowed. Due to past *karma*, the parents are fated to undergo the type of sorrow caused by having a widowed daughter. The daughter, due to her past *karma*, is fated to suffer widowhood. In both cases, you have two sets of individual *karmas* that are linked together.

It is like demand and supply. For instance, the Manager of a company wishes to recruit someone to fill a particular position. He is looking for a certain type of person with certain type of qualifications for the post. So he advertises, interviews and finally selects the one whom he thinks is suitable for the post. That person has the necessary qualifications to satisfy the Manager's requirements. One has the requirements, the other has the requisites and both are mutually satisfied. So, it is a case of demand and supply. In the previous two examples also, the same principle applies. The Law of *Karma* is thus very scientific and mathematical.

S - Baba, what about the relationship between husband and wife?

SAI - Your past karma determines the type of life-partner you have in the present birth. Your *karma* dictates whether or not you will be happy in your marriage.

S - But there are many instances when a good wife has a bad husband and vice versa.

SAI - That again is due to past *karma*. For example, take the case of Ravana. He was an asura with demonic qualities. Yet his wife Mandodari was a very *sathwic* woman. She was a pati-vrata. Why, then, this imbalance? Now, Ravana was actually a great devotee of Lord Shiva in his previous birth, but due to a momentary lapse of good conduct, he was condemned to be born as an asura in his next birth. His devotion and good deeds in the previous birth earned him a good and noble wife and the good fortune of dying at the Hands of Sri Rama Himself. Likewise, Mandodari's past *karma* was responsible for her getting an asuric husband, although in that birth itself she was of noble character.

S - Do divorce and separation affect *karmic* debt, Baba?

SAI - Two people come together because of their past *karma* and the *karmic* debt owing to each other. Once the obligations are fulfilled and the debts are mutually cancelled, they will be separated by the natural occurrence of death. Death is the natural act. Divorce and separation are unnatural acts. They are man-made and not God-made. If two people decide to separate, they will be doing so while the *karmic* debt between them still exists. This debt will have to be repaid as it is the Law of *Karma*. So, it will be carried over to the next birth, when the two people will have to work off the mutual debt and cancel it completely.

S - Why are people born physically handicapped and mentally retarded, Baba?

SAI - In previous births, such people would have been completely amoral, with no standards of right or wrong, of good or bad. Their moral codes would have been very low and they would have engaged in acts of moral degeneracy and decadence. Such people will be re-born with physical and mental afflictions and will suffer in this way for past misdeeds.

S - What about still born children, Baba?

SAI - They are so born because their *karma* stipulates that they have only a few months left in the physical world in which to work off their *karmic* debt. They are actually highly enlightened souls who finish their *karma* in these few months and depart. They will not be born again. The parents of such children should really consider themselves fortunate and blessed.

S - Nowadays, we see so many cases of good people suffering while the bad ones prosper. How would you explain this, Baba?

SAI - The good people suffer now because of some bad *karma* in the previous birth. And the wicked ones prosper on account of some good which they did in the previous birth.

S - But the so-called wicked people in the present birth must have been reasonably good in their previous birth in order to have performed good *karma*. How is it that they are re-born with lesser moral values?

SAI - People are neither wholly good nor wholly bad. There is a potential saint in every sinner and a potential sinner in every saint. Take Valmeeki, for instance. He was the notorious bandit Ratnakara, but he was overcome by remorse, repented, did penance and was transformed into the renowned sage. So also, good persons perform good deeds according to their nature. But one evil impulse on their part will cause a momentary lapse in their moral code and may lead to a bad or wrong action. This will cancel some of the good they have done. For example, the great sage Vishwamitra achieved great Yogic powers through dhyana and tapas. But he also had a vice, a bad temper which he was unable to conquer. When provoked, he uttered a curse and by doing this he exhausted the power he had gained. So, he had to start all over again from the beginning. Thus, good persons may do a lot of good but one terrible lapse will cause their downfall. When they are born again, there will be a slight deterioration of virtues and morals; but at the same time they will continue to enjoy the fruits of their good actions in the past.

However, when you talk of people "prospering" and enjoying "prosperity", you are really referring to material and worldly prosperity. But how do you know whether these people have "prosperity of the heart"? Do they have real happiness? Of course not, for money cannot give you the lasting happiness that morality and faith can. Money comes and goes but morality comes and grows. A person may be financially rich but spiritually poor. In the eyes of God, it is not the financial bank balance which counts but the spiritual bank balance.

S - When good people undergo suffering and misfortunes, are they solely the result of past *karma*, Baba? Or, are they tests meted out by God?

SAI - If those persons are also sincere devotees, then sometimes God sends them troubles to test the strength of their devotion. If the devotees realize that the main objective of man is not to be reborn again and again and if they are striving towards this objective, they will be beset with untold miseries and sufferings as a means of burning away all the karmas of past births. This is all according to the Judgement and Grace of God.

S - Does retribution set in immediately, Baba?

SAI - Every action has an equal and opposite reaction. If you throw a ball against the wall, it immediately bounces back to you. The more forceful the throw, the more forceful is the rebounce. Retribution depends on the nature of the action performed. For example, if you lose your temper and shout at somebody, you may suffer instant retribution by banging your leg or stubbing your toe. Even if you have a bad thought in your mind, it rebounds on you in some way, though you may not realize it as such.

There are cases where people are constantly engaged in misdeeds like dishonest actions, physical and mental *himsa* and so on. Sooner or later, they will have to pay for their wrong deeds. A thief, for example, will go on committing thefts but at some time or the other, he will be caught and he will have to pay for his crimes. A person may go on performing evil acts till his day of death, but he cannot escape his payment. If he does not pay fully in this birth, he will do so in the next.

However, a person may realize his mistakes. Overcome by remorse, he sincerely repents for his past misdeeds and tries to atone for them. In that case, he will make his payment in the same birth itself. It will not be carried over to the next.

S - Can repentance mitigate suffering, Baba?

SAI - Of course. Repentance, prayaschit, sadhana - all these can mitigate or reduce the suffering caused by past *karmas*. They cannot cancel out the karma but they can lessen the burden of *karma*. It is like being given a very bitter medicine to drink. By itself it is too bitter to take but if you dilute it with water or mix it with sugar, it will not seem so unbearable. Likewise, you can dilute your suffering with the help of sadhana, japa, dhyana, bhajan, namasmarana, etc. They cannot completely wipe out past *karma* because the consequences of *karma* have to be faced. They cannot be avoided for that is *Karmic* Law. But bhakti and sadhana can make karma sit lightly on you.

S - Doesn't God's Grace have anything to do with it?

SAI - Naturally it does. A sincere sadhaka will draw down the Grace of God and earn His Blessings. God's Grace will act as a sort of tranquilliser or pain-killer. Thereby, the pain will not be felt much although it is gone through. The Grace of God is the ultimate deciding factor. If the sadhaka is sincere and has sraddha and ekagratha (steadfastness and single pointedness), God may even decide to bless him by wiping out his past *karma*. It is like a prisoner being let off earlier on account of his good behaviour while he is in jail. God, therefore, is the Ultimate Judge. In cases He thinks fit, He may by His Grace and Compassion, transcend all the laws of karma. But this happens very rarely as God does not usually interfere with *Karmic* Law.

S - Baba, what are *sahaja karma* and *asahaja karma*?

SAI - Natural and unnatural *karma*. *Sahaja karma* or natural *karma* is *swadharma*, that is *karma* which is natural to one's birth, duty and occupation. (*Karma* in this case refers to action). For example, it is the duty of a soldier to fight. That is his *swadharma* or *sahaja karma* and killing is part of his duty. But a civilian has no right to fight and kill. If he does so, he will be arrested and put in jail. His act is *asahaja karma* or unnatural *karma* because it is not in keeping with his *dharma* and duty.

Take another example. In a court of law, the judge listens to the arguments of the prosecutor and the defense counsel and then passes the verdict on the prisoner. It may be a verdict of imprisonment, life-sentence or death. Whatever it is, his action is swadharma and is natural to his occupation and duty. Delivering judgements is his occupation and duty. It is sahaja karma and he will not be bound by it. So long as his verdict is impartial and fair and so long as his judgement is based purely on the guilt or innocence of the prisoner, he will not be bound by his action. Instead, if the judge passes a verdict of guilt and sentences the prisoner to imprisonment, or death purely because of personal malice, hatred or vendetta, though he knows that the prisoner is actually innocent, then the judge is engaging in asahaja karma or unnatural *karma*. This act will go against him and he will have to suffer the consequences some time. So you see, it is the motive which is important. It is the motive or the impulse behind the action which determines whether the action is sahaja or asahaja, natural or unnatural.

Again, it is the teacher's duty to punish the pupil for misconduct and misbehaviour. That is natural *karma*. But if the teacher punishes the pupil simply because he does not like him, it becomes unnatural *karma*. So, it is the motive which decides whether karma is *sahaja* or *asahaja*. *Sahaja karma* will not cause impulses for rebirth. It is not binding on a person. But *asahaja karma* leads to action and reaction and thereby to birth and rebirth.

However, once you realize that you are not the doer but only the witness and surrender all acts to the Feet of the Lord, you have nothing to fear. All acts will be carried out by you for the sake of God and so you will automatically do only what is good and what is right. Do your best and leave the rest. He will take care of everything. That is the correct attitude.

S - Baba, will you please explain the difference between *prarabdha karma, sanchita karma* and *agami karma*.

SAI - What is prarabdha? Prarabdha means prarambha, the beginning of your fate which chains you in the cycle of joy and sorrow, in the cycle of birth and death. Sanchita is the past, prarabdha is the present and agami is the future *karma*.

Sanchita karma is the combination of all your samskaras (your thoughts, values, qualities, character, words, actions, etc) - in your previous births. It consists of good and bad *samskaras*. *Sanchita karma* is the cause of rebirth and determines future births.

Prarabdha karma is the consequence of all your previous *samskaras*. What you are going through now is *prarabdha* and it is the result of your samskaras in the past births. *Prarabdha karma* depends upon and is determined by *sanchita karma*. If your sanchita was good, your prarabdha will be good; if your sanchita was bad, your prarabdha will also be bad. No one can escape prarabdha because no one can escape the consequences or the fruits of one's actions and *karmas*. However, even if your prarabdha is not good, it can be mitigated by prayer, sadhana and the Grace of God.

Agami karma is your future *karma*. While *prarabdha karma* is not in your hands, *agami karma* is. You can atleast learn the lesson in this birth that you reap what you sow. Prarabdha is the result of what you have already sowed in previous births. You cannot undo it and must accept it bravely and cheerfully. But *agami karma* is very much in your hands and its course can be determined by you right now, in your present birth. By engaging in good *karmas* and by leading a life based on morality and righteousness, you can ensure for yourself a good life in the future.

So, be good, do good, see good, hear good, speak good, think good. Then, God's Grace will always be with you and you need have no fear of any *karmas*.

AUM SHANTI SHANTI SHANTIH:

A

GARLAND OF LOVE

AN ODE TO MY BELOVED SAI

I want to find a special greeting and gift for you,
For the usual common ones won't do.
I want to sing a song in Your praise,
But no mortal tune can extol Your Grace.
I want to write a sonnet on Your Glory,
But can find no words in this earthly repertory.
I want to compose a poem on Your Majesty,
But no rhyme on earth can portray Your Divinity.
I want to paint a picture of Your Living Incarnation,
But no worldly colours can capture Your Wondrous
    Vision.

I want to give You my heart,
But I find it's already in Your keeping.
I want to give You my love,
But You already stole it and left me yearning.
I want to give You myself and all that's mine,
But find that no longer am "I" but Thine!
What then is left in this empty human shell?
Silent adoration and devotion most profound,
Mute love, worship and trust, firm and sound-
Yes, whatever may come, these do abound;
With them will my heart and mind sweetly resound.

A PRAYER FOR REBIRTH

Wither am I going? What am I seeking?
Like a ship floundering on stormy seas,
Tossed and turned by the waves and tides,
Struggling helplessly to reach the shores.
Like a child lost in the dark wilds,
Running aimlessly, crying piteously,
Searching in vain for a glimmer of light.
Even so am I, your lonely devotee
Wandering in the gloom; a waif
Caught in the web of toil and strife.
The aim forgotten, the path mistaken
The mind with hazy clouds begotten.
Bemused, benumbed, befogged;
Yet, with spirit left to mourn
          "Where am I going?
          What am I seeking?
          Wither am I turning?"
Thus do I turn to Thee,
My beloved Lord and Master,
My Redeemer, Guide and Protector.
Hear my plea, my impassioned plea!
Clear the cobwebs from my mind,
Lift the veil that obscures my vision
And teach me anew my life's first mission.
Set my eyes on that, my just target
And place my feet on the desired road.
As yet another morrow makes a start,
Let it awaken within my heart
The dawn of new hope, vision and zest;
So that once more will I with measured tread

Venture along the pious pilgrimage,
And win again Thy Blessings and Thy Grace,
Thy Love that radiates from Thy Divine Face.

I NEED THEE!

As a temple without bells,
As a ship without sails,
As a lock without a key,
So am I without Thee.
I need Thee, O! Sai!

As a rose without perfume,
As a lamp without oil,
As a shore without sea,
So am I without Thee.
I need Thee, Beloved Sai!

Thou art my companion on the path of life,
In all the mutations of time and births.
Thou wilt never lose hold of me
And I am Thine for ever and ever more.

THE THOUGHT OF YOU

The thought of You runs through my days -
A thread of gold that glints and gleams.
The thought of You is never gone even when I weave
    my web of dreams.
The thought of You brings out the sun when shadows
    fall around my path,
It is the road that leads me homeward and the flame that
    warms my heart.

The thought of You is my lodestar, my shining beacon of
    light,
It is my sheet anchor, the guiding lamp that helps me see
    aright.
You are my life, You are my sight,
You are my love, my hope and reason bright.
O' Sai, Most Dearly Beloved, what more can I say or tell
Except that You have the core of me, the world has only
    the shell.

A PRAYER FOR PEACE

Baba My Lord, most gentle and kind,
Give me bliss and tranquillity of mind.
A heart content
With all at peace.
Lead me, O' Sai, down quiet ways;
My soul sustain,
My faith increase.
Give me a calm and steadfast will
To meet whatever is to be,
Facing the future unafraid
With courage and serenity.

SURRENDER

Baba! I give You myself -
These faults and vices ten score and nine,
Take them, take them all for they are not mine.
I give You this EGO, this deadly and vicious arrogance -
It's a relentless barrier between me and your Effulgence.

I give You this MIND, this wretched tangle of confusion
It weaves a web of smoke, clouding my inner vision.
I give You these THOUGHTS, these desires countless
   and wayward,
They are like blinding dust, stopping me seek inward.
I give You my KARMAS, past, present and future -
They sit on me like an unshakable vesture.
I give You my THOUGHTS, WORDS AND DEEDS
      in score -
They are poisonous darts reaching to the very core.
I give you this INTELLECT with its logic, reason, cold
      and clear -
It keeps me away from You, my love, my very dear.
Baba Sai! I do not want these for they are not mine;
Take them all and destroy them with Your Will Divine.
Make me pure of body, mind and heart,
Soft and white like butter and curd -
For the only thing I truly desire is You,
   My Precious Lord!

AUM SHANTI SHANTI SHANTIH :

GLOSSARY

Adwaita	-	The Philosophy of Monism or Non-duality which believes in the one-ness and unity of everything. The individual soul is a part of the Univer-sal Soul and will ultimately merge in it. This theory was first propoun-ded by Sri Sankaracharya in the 8th century A.D.
Ahimsa	-	Non-Violence
Ajna	-	Command, order
Antar Vani	-	Inner Voice
Arjuna	-	The third Pandava brother whose Divine father was Indra, the King of the Gods. Arjuna was famed for his skill in archery.
Asuras	-	Demons of the first order who were in constant hostility with the Gods.
Atma	-	Soul
Avatar	-	Incarnation of God.
Avidya	-	Ignorance.
Bhagavad Gita	-	The Divine Song of God. It was taught by Sri Krishna to Arjuna on the battle field of Kurukshetra. Sage Vyasa later rendered it in the form of a book consisting of eighteen chapters. The Gita is the holy book of the Hindus.
Bhajan	-	Song in praise of God.

Bhakti	-	Love, attachment and devotion towards God.
Bheeshma	-	The son of Shantanu by the river Goddess Ganga; he was invincible in martial arts and was the Guru in these arts to the Kaurava and Pandava Princes. He was their grand-sire.
Bhogis	-	People with worldly attachments; those who indulge in pleasures.
Bhoktha	-	The one who enjoys or consumes.
Brahman	-	The Universal Consciousness; the Supreme Eternal Being.
Brahma jnani	-	A saint who has spiritual wisdom and Divine knowledge.
Chaitanya	-	The Universal Consciousness, the Universal Soul, the Highest Knowledge.
Chith	-	Knowledge, awareness.
Chitha	-	Mind (manas).
Chitha Suddhi	-	Purification of the mind.
Datha	-	The one who gives or bestows.
Dharma	-	Righteousness, code of conduct, religion.
Dhritarashtra	-	Brother of Pandu and the blind ruler of Hastinapur (in the Dwapara Yuga). He had hundred sons called the Kauravas, by his wife Gandhari.
Dhyana	-	Meditation.
Draupadi	-	The dark-skinned daughter of King Drupada of Panchala and wife of the Pandava brothers.

Drishti	-	Sight, vision, perception.
Dwaita	-	The Philosophy of Dualism which is based on the belief that the individual self is different and distinct from the Universal Soul. This theory was first propounded by Sri Madhavacharya.
Ekagratha	-	One - pointedness, single-mindedness.
Gandhari	-	The wife of the blind King Dhritarashtra of Hastinapur. She was a very chaste and noble woman. Be cause her husband was blind, she spent her life blindfolded.
Guna	-	Quality, attribute, characteristic.
Guru	-	Master, teacher, guide. The word "Guru" means one who dispels ignorance.
Hiranya Garbha	-	The Golden Womb; the primal cosmic sphere which, splitting in two, was the cause of creation.
Hiranyakasipu	-	The demon king and father of the great devotee Prahlada. He was an atheist and was eventually killed by Lord Vishnu who took the form of Narasimha (half-man and half-lion).

Indriyas	-	The senses. There are five senses of knowledge called Jnanendriyas (the eyes, ears, tongue, nose and skin), and five senses of action called karmendriyas (the hands, legs, vocal organs, genitals and excretory organs).
Japa	-	Repetition or recitation of God's Name.
Jnana	-	Knowledge, Wisdom.
Jnana-swaroopa	-	Embodiment of Knowledge.
Jnanendriyas	-	See *Indriyas*.
Jnani	-	One who has acquired knowledge and wisdom.
Kaalateeta	-	One who is above and beyond Time (God).
Kali Yuga	-	The Iron Age. It is the fourth and the present age of creation. It began in 3102 B.C and will last 432,000 years after which the universal cycle will re-commence.
Karma	-	Action, fate, destiny.
Karmendriyas	-	See *Indriyas*.
Kartha	-	The one who does, who performs.
Kauravas	-	The hundred sons of Dhritarashtra and Gandhari. They symbolise unrighteousness and wickedness.

Krishna	-	The eighth Incarnation of Lord Vishnu, who took birth in the Dwaparayuga (the third age in the cycle of creation). He took birth in order to foster Shanti and Prema (Peace and Love).
Kurukshetra	-	The battlefield where the Pandavas and Kauravas fought the historical Mahabharata war which can be dated sometime between 3500 BC and 3100 BC. The battle symbolises the fight between the good and evil forces in our own body.
Mandodari	-	The chaste and noble wife of Ravana, the King of Lanka. Though her husband was a demon, she was extremely loyal and devoted to him.
Maya	-	Illusion; delusion.
Mithya	-	Unreal; apparent; seeming.
Namasmarana	-	Contemplation of God's Name.
Nithya	-	Eternal; permanent; lasting.
Om	-	The Primeval sound of creation.
Panchabhuthas	-	The five elements of creation - earth, water, fire, wind and sky.

Pandavas	-	The five sons of King Pandu through his two wives Kunti and Madri. The Pandavas symbolise goodness and the five divine quali-ties of Sathya, Dharma, Shanti, Prema and Ahimsa (Truth, Righte--ousness, Peace, Love and Non-violence)
Parasurama	-	The sixth incarnation of Lord Vishnu and Bheeshma's Guru in martial arts and warfare.
Patanjali	-	The foremost exponent of Yoga. His date is unknown though many scholars assign him to the 2nd century B.C. His "Yoga Sutras" are the main source of the Yoga system of philosophy in India.
Pati-Vrata	-	A chaste and virtuous wife, truly and completely devoted to her husband.
Prahlada	-	Son of the demon king Hiranya-kasipu. He was a great devotee of Lord Vishnu.
Prayaschit	-	Atonement, expiation of one's sins.
Rajas/rajasic	-	Passionate, dynamic and active disposition which includes qualities like egoism, arrogance, anger, pride conceit, etc.

Rama	-	The seventh Incarnation of Lord Vishnu who took birth in the Treta yuga (the second age in the cycle of creation). His wife was Sita. He fostered the principles of Sathya and Dharma (Truth and Righteousness).
Ravana	-	The demon King of Lanka. He abducted Sita and forced Lord Rama to wage a war against him. He was finally killed by Rama.
Rishis	-	Sages, Saints.
Rogis	-	People who are sickly and are stricken with ill-health.
Sadguru	-	The Greatest Teacher or Master (God)
Sadhana	-	Spiritual practice and austerity; spiritual discipline.
Sadhaka	-	One who is engaged in spiritual discipline and practice.
Samskaras	-	One's collective thoughts, actions, qualities, character, morals, desires, ambitions etc. which one accumulates over a series of births.
Sathsang	-	The company of the good, the wise and the saintly.
Sathwa/sathwic	-	Balanced, regulated and moderate disposition which includes qualities like equanimity, love, compassion, tolerance, generosity, etc.
Seva	-	Service, help, assistance.

Sishya	-	Pupil, student.
Soham	-	Sanskrit word meaning "I am He".
Sraddha	-	Interest, steadfastness, tenacity.
Suddhi	-	Purification, cleansing.
Swadharma	-	One's own duty; duty which is natural to one's birth, occupation or position.
Tamas/tamasic	-	Dull, inactive and lethargic disposition which includes qualities like sloth, laziness, meanness, envy, jealousy etc.
Thyaga	-	Sacrifice, renunciation.
Thyagaraja	-	A renowned saint of South India (1767-1847) and a great exponent of classical Carnatic music. He was an ardent devotee of Lord Rama and composed about 24,000 songs in praise of Him.
Trikarana	-	The three instruments : hands, tongue and mind.
Trikarana Suddhi	-	Purification of the three instruments (hands, tongue and mind).
Upavasa	-	Fasting, nearness or closeness to God.
Vairagya	-	Detachment or non-attachment to worldly and sensual objects.
Valmeeki	-	The great sage and author of the epic poem "Ramayana" (The story of Rama). He was one of the seven sages.

Vichaara	-	Examination, inquiry, analysis.
Vishwamitra	-	A renowned king turned sage; he became one of the seven great sages by the strength of his penances and meditations.
Viveka	-	Discrimination; differentiation between right and wrong, truth and untruth, reality and unreality, etc.
Yoga	-	One of the systems of Hindu philosophy involving physical and mental discipline. Yoga means "Union with God".
Yogis	-	Ascetics; those who practise Yoga.
Yuga	-	A cycle of creation which constitutes 4,320,000 human years. There are four yugas or ages - Krita, Treta, Dwapara and Kali. We are now in the last Yuga.

OUR PUBLICATIONS

01.70 QS & AS. ON PRACTICAL SPIRITUALITY
   AND SATHYA SAI BABA   - O.P.Vidyakar   Rs. 90
02.A JOURNEY TO LOVE (Fourth Edition)   - David Bailey   Rs.180
03.A JOURNEY TO LOVE (Spanish)   - David Bailey   Rs.375
04.ANOTHER JOURNEY TO LOVE   - Faye Bailey   Rs.350
05."ALEX" THE DOLPHIN   - Light Strom   Rs. 90
06.A STORY OF INDIA AND
   PATAL BHUVANESWAR   - Jennifer Warren   Rs. 60
07.A COMPENDIUM OF THE TEACHINGS OF
   SATHYA SAI BABA (Second Edition)   - Charlene Leslie-Chadan Rs.555
08.ASHES,ASHES WE ALL FALL DOWN   - Gloria St. John   Rs. 80
09.BAPU TO BABA   - V.K. Narasimhan   Rs.120
10.BHAGAVAN SRI SATHYA SAI BABA
   DISCOURSES IN KODAIKANAL, APRIL 96 - Pooja Kapahi   Rs.120
11.BUDO-KA-TRUE SPIRITUAL WARRIORS   - Deena Naidu   Rs.200
12. CRICKET FOR LOVE - A Souvenir on Sri Sathya Sai Unity Cup   Rs.250
13.CUTTING THE TIES THAT BIND   - Phyllis Krystal   Rs.110
14.CUTTING MORE TIES THAT BIND   - Phyllis Krystal   Rs.120
15.CUTTING THE TIES THAT BIND
   - WORK BOOK   - Phyllis Krystal   Rs.140
16.DA PUTTAPARTHI
   A PATAL BHUVANESHWAR (Italian)   - Sandra Percy   Rs.150
17.DEATHING (Indian Edition)   - Anya Foos-Graber   Rs.195
18.DISCOVERING MARTIAL ARTS   - Deena Naidu   Rs.265
19.DIVINE LEELAS OF BHAGAVAN
   SRI SATHYA SAI BABA   - Nagamani Purnaiya   Rs. 90
20.EDUCATION IN HUMAN VALUES (3 Vols.) - June Auton   Rs.750
21.GLIMPSES OF THE DIVINE   - Birgitte Rodriguez   Rs.150
22.GOOD CHANCES (Second Edition)   - Howard Levin   Rs.120
23.GOD AND HIS GOSPEL   - Dr. M.N.Rao   Rs.120
24.GOD DESCENDS ON EARTH   - Sanjay Kant   Rs. 60
25.GOD LIVES IN INDIA   - R. K. Karanjia   Rs. 75
26.HEART TO HEART (Reprint)   - Howard Levin   Rs.120
27.IN QUEST OF GOD   - P.P. Arya   Rs.120
28.KNOW THYSELF (Second Edition)   - Gerard T. Satvic   Rs.180
29.LET ME SOW LOVE   - Doris May Gibson   Rs.120
30.LETTERS FROM A GRANDFATHER   - S. K. Bose   Rs.180
31.MESSAGES (JAPANEESE)   - Dr. M.N. Rao   Rs.150
32.MIRACLES ARE MY VISITING CARDS   - Erlendur Haraldsson   Rs. 180
33.MOHANA BALA SAI (Children's Book)   - Sai Mira   Rs.120
34.MUKTI THE LION FINDS HIMSELF   - Gina Suritsch   Rs. 85
35.MESSAGES FROM MY DEAREST
   FRIEND SAI BABA   - Elvie Bailey   Rs.130
36.NARA NARAYANA GUFA ASHRAM Part III - Swami Maheswaranand Rs. 20
37.PRASANTHI GUIDE   - R. Padmanaban   Rs. 50
38.SAI BABA GITA   - Al Drucker   Rs.240
39.SAI BABA: THE ETERNAL COMPANION   - B. P. Misra   Rs.100
40.SELF REALISATION   - Al Drucker   Rs. 35
41.SATVIC FOOD & HEALTH (2nd Rev. Edition) - Gerard T. Satvic   Rs. 40
42.SAI SANDESH   - Sai Usha   Rs. 50
43.SAI MY DIVINE BELOVED   - Sai Usha   Rs. 50

FORTHCOMING PUBLICATIONS ...

Postal Charges

India: At the rate of 50 ps. per 100 gms plus Rs.12/- for Registration. Maximum 5 kg per parcel. Packing and Forwarding Charges per parcel Rs.40/-

Overseas: **Sea Mail** to North America, South America, Europe Rs.171/- for a 5 kg parcel, Singapore, Malaysia, New Zealand & Australia Rs.147/- plus packing and forwarding Rs.60/- per parcel

Air Mail Minimum postal Charges Rs.171/- per parcel to North and South America and Europe and Rs.147/- for Singapore, Malaysia, New Zealand and ustralia plus Rs.3/- for every 20 gms. Packing and forwarding charge Rs.60/- per parcel.

We accept your mail orders against bank drafts and credit cards.
Bank drafts should be drawn in favour of Sri Sathya Sai Towers Hotels P Ltd and payable in India.

✁ —

To
Sri Sathya Sai Towers Hotels P Ltd.,
3/497 Main Road,
Prasanthi Nilayam 515 134, India

Dear Sir,
I herewith enclose the list of books required along with advance payment in full including postage and packing. Please despatch at your earliest

☐ Enclosed Bank draft for Rs................

☐ Charge the total amount Rs................ ticked below to my Credit Card

     ☐ *Visa*   ☐ *Mastercard*   ☐ *Diners Club*

Card No ☐☐☐☐ ☐☐☐☐ ☐☐☐☐ ☐☐☐☐

                                                   M M DD Y Y
Card Expiry Date.........................   Date of Birth ☐☐ ☐☐ ☐☐

Card Members Signature.......................................

Name: Mr./Ms._____
Address_____
City_____Country_____
Phone: _____ Fax: _____
E-mail:_____